ODD MOMENTS IN BASEBALL

JOEL COHEN
Illustrations by Tom Payne

SCHOLASTIC INC.
New York   Toronto   London   Auckland   Sydney
Mexico City   New Delhi   Hong Kong

*To all the moms and dads
and daughters and sons (mine included)
for whom baseball—in all its splendor
and quirkiness—has been a supreme
bonding experience.*

Many people—baseball league and
team staff members, former players, and
editors, sportscasters and columnists—
should be credited with assists in
the making of this book. Space doesn't
permit naming all of them, but deserving
of special mention are Amy Goehner,
James Kim, Chris Leible, Tony Morante,
Phil Mushnick, Bart Swain and Sal Yvars.
To them and those unamed,
my sincere gratitude.

ISBN 0-590-37066-9

12 11 10 9 8 7 6 5 4 3 2 1   0 1 2 3 4 5 6/0

Printed in the U.S.A.
First Scholastic printing, March 2000
Book Design: Michael Malone

CONTENTS

INTRODUCTION

Just
because
professional
baseball players are
highly skilled doesn't mean
they're perfect. They have their
share of goof-ups, crazy quirks, wacky
superstitions, and odd moments. They experience
strange twists of fate, lucky and unlucky bounces, and
plays that go haywire. All of this contributes to our
enjoyment of the sport they play.
This book is all about the bizarre real-life
characters and funny incidents that
have helped make baseball
so entertaining. Hope
you enjoy
them.

CHAPTER 1

ANYTHING FOR A WIN

The goal of players, coaches, and managers is to get a win for their team. Sometimes they'll do just about anything for a victory. In the past, attempts to get ahead have included tampering with equipment, intimidation tactics, bizarre strategies—even spying on the other team!

Snow Problem!

In the 1950s, the New York Giants and Cleveland Indians often played against each other in preseason games. One year, the teams played in Denver, just three days after a huge snowstorm had hit the city. By game time the sun had come out, and the snow had been plowed and piled near the outfield fence. It was decided that all balls hit into the snow near the outfield fence would be called ground-rule doubles.

With two outs, an Indian slugger drove a long fly to right center between Artie Wilson and speedy center fielder Bobby Thomson. In a flash, Thomson leaped and appeared to have caught the ball. In truth, the ball got past him! Unseen by the umpires, Wilson quickly made a snowball and flipped it to Thomson, who triumphantly held it up in his glove as if he'd caught the third out. He raced to the dugout, inning over. From the bench, the Giants rolled a baseball to the mound, as if it were the one Thomson had "caught."

The real ball was never found.

No Way to Treat a Ball

Pitchers will try almost anything to gain an advantage over a batter. All sorts of devices and techniques have been used.

Balls have been scuffed up by just about everything from sandpaper and spikes to belt buckles and diamond rings. Sometimes baseballs were stored in the ice box to "deaden" them. Over the years players and coaches have applied saliva, mud, petroleum, licorice, or tobacco juice to make the balls move in mysterious (and hard-to-hit!) ways.

Covering All the Possibilities

Charles O. Finley, the outrageous owner of the Oakland A's, used to cover all the bases. For example, he timed his pitchers to make sure they weren't slowing down games by taking too long between pitches. In 1974, he hired a track sprinter, Herb

Washington, to be a pinch runner. Finley even hired an astrologist to help with the team's fortunes.

With $300 bonuses, Finley encouraged his players to grow thick mustaches and heavy sideburns, presumably to make them look more intimidating. In fact, the Oakland A's *were* intimidating. They won three straight World Series in the 1970s (beating the Reds in 1972, the Mets in 1973, and the Dodgers in 1974).

The Last Resort

Sometimes pitchers resorted to fairly drastic measures.

Dazzy Vance, who was with the Brooklyn Dodgers in the 1920s and early 1930s, was pitching in a scoreless game against the St. Louis Cardinals at Brooklyn's Ebbets Field.

The Cardinal runner on third, Sparky Adams, took off and was about to steal home. Thinking quickly, Dazzy did the only thing he could think of to prevent the runner from scoring: He aimed the ball directly at the batter, Chick Hafey, and struck him!

Because of the hit batsman, the umpire ruled the ball dead and Adams had to go back to third. The scoreless tie continued into the tenth inning, when the Cardinals scored the game's only run.

Pining for a Home Run

In late July 1983, the New York Yankees were playing the Kansas City Royals when George Brett hit a two-run, ninth-inning home run with two outs, giving the Royals a 5–4 lead. But Billy Martin, the Yankees manager, argued that Brett's bat had pine tar on it that extended six inches beyond the 17-inch legal limit. The umpires ruled Brett out and the game was over, with the Yankees victorious, 4–3.

The Royals protested and, later that week, the president of the American League, Lee MacPhail, upheld the protest on grounds that the rules stated only that the bat be removed from the game. The home run was reinstated. But the final four outs (one for Kansas City and three for the Yankees) would have to be replayed later in the season.

There was tremendous interest in the controversy. A Kansas City publisher even issued bumper stickers with the slogan, "I Pine for George." However, another George—George Steinbrenner, owner of the Yankees—said, "It is against our wishes to play [the game]." Still, the game was scheduled to resume on August 18 (which was supposed to have been a day off).

But the main character in the drama would not be playing in the resumed contest.

Furious at the initial decision that his home run didn't count, Brett had been ejected from the original game for his "aggressive behavior" toward the umpires. Also thrown out were Kansas City manager Dick Howser, coach Rocky Colavito, and pitcher Gaylord Perry (who had tried to pass Brett's bat through the dugout to the Royals clubhouse).

The resumed Yankees–Royals contest began with the Royals leading, 5–4. There were two outs and the bases were empty. It lasted less than ten minutes, and was played before only 1,245 fans (compared with 33,944 at the original game). Three young fans had sued the Yankees for the right to see the resumed game without having to pay another admission, and two hours before game time, the Yankees announced they would honor rainchecks from the original game. Apparently, not many heard the announcement.

In any case, those who did attend watched four hitters in a row (one Royal, then three Yankees) make out. The Royals won, 5–4, by George, on Brett's disputed homer hit 25 days earlier.

The Excuse Was a Corker

Filling bats with foreign substances like cork is a definite no-no. Sure, it helps the ball go farther—but it's against the rules. Still, some players may feel that rules are made to be broken. When Cincinnati Reds third baseman Chris Sabo's bat broke during a game in Cincinnati, on July 29, 1996, it exposed loads of cork.

Claiming that he couldn't possibly have put the cork in the bat, he offered several possible alibis, including the excuse, "I can barely change a lightbulb." And then, referring to the fact that he had only three home runs and 16 RBIs for the season, he stated, "That's hardly an endorsement of the cork industry."

Who's That Masked Manager?

When a manager gets ejected from a game, he's supposed to stay out of the dugout. But shortly after New York Mets manager Bobby Valentine was tossed out of a game against the Toronto Blue Jays on June 9, 1999, a mysterious figure appeared in the dugout. He was wearing a coat, dark sunglasses, and what turned out to be a fake mustache. The mystery man turned out to be Valentine.

He was suspended for two games and fined $5,000 for violating baseball rule 5.1. Valentine claimed he did it to lighten things up for his team, which went on to win the game in 14 innings, 4–3.

Big Train

Hall of Famer Walter "Big Train" Johnson, of the Washington Senators, threw so hard, one batter gave up after two strikes, telling the umpire that Johnson could *have* the third strike.

Johnson also had superb control; batters could stand in against him confident they wouldn't be hit. One time in Detroit, the Tigers had the bases loaded with none out, and Johnson struck out Ty Cobb, Bobby Veach, and Sam Crawford, three left-handed batters, on nine pitches.

Johnson once came into a ballgame in the ninth inning and shut out the Philadelphia Athletics until the 19th inning when his catcher got hurt. The replacement back-stop, Rip Williams, couldn't hold Johnson's first pitch. The ball clipped plate umpire Billy Evans on the ear, causing it to bleed. "You're not gonna get me killed," the umpire complained to Williams, and called the game on account of darkness—even though it was only about 4:30 in the afternoon!

The next day, Johnson relieved against the A's again, this time in the eighth inning with the score tied. He pitched scoreless ball until the 21st inning, when his team finally scored to win 4–3. So in two days— against what many consider the greatest team of its time—"Big Train" Johnson pitched 26 innings without allowing a run.

In Cahoots

Ty Cobb of the Detroit Tigers was one of history's greatest baseball players and also one of the most hated. He was a win-at-any-cost competitor—even if it meant deliberately injuring an opponent. Which does a lot to explain the following story.

As the 1910 baseball season drew to a close, Cobb was in a close batting race with Nap Lajoie of the Cleveland Indians. Trying to keep the hated Cobb from winning the title, St. Louis Browns manager Jack O'Connor and coach Harry Howell instructed rookie third baseman Red Corriden to play deep at third each time Lajoie batted in a doubleheader.

With the third baseman back, Nap was able to beat out seven bunts, six of them in a row. Coincidentally, a St. Louis outfielder also "lost" one of Lajoie's balls in the sun. The result: Lajoie had eight hits in eight times at bat. (After the season, O'Connor and Howell were barred from Major League jobs for the orders they'd given.)

Despite the Browns' gifts to Lajoie, Cobb still won the batting title, .385 to Lajoie's .384. Then in 1981, *The Sporting News* discovered an error had been made in calculating Cobb's average (a game in which Cobb went 2-for-3 had counted twice). In fact, Cobb had really hit only .383. But Commissioner Bowie Kuhn and a committee ruled that the error would not be corrected. Cobb's 1910 batting title still stands.

Mind Games

The morning of the first game of the 1927 World Series at Forbes Field in Pittsburgh, members of the Pittsburgh Pirates filed into the stands to watch their American League rivals, the New York Yankees, take batting practice.

Realizing the Pirates would be watching, Yankee manager Miller Huggins had an idea. He assigned his ace pitcher, Waite Hoyt, to pitch batting practice. Waite was told to throw hard and fast—but right over the plate.

So the Yankee hitters, known as "Murderers Row" for their batting power, kept belting shots over the fences. After watching the mighty display of Babe Ruth, Lou Gehrig, Bob Meusel, and Tony Lazzeri, Pirate hitting stars Paul and Lloyd Waner just shook their heads and left the stands.

Whether or not it was due to the devastating psychological effect of their powerful display during batting practice, the Yankees took the Series, four games to none.

Throw It Away

Some players take an odd delight in negative accomplishments. For instance, in a game in May 1948, Boston Red Sox rookie pitcher Mickey McDermott and veteran Mickey Harris had tied a record by walking a combined 17 Cleveland Indians.

There were two outs in the ninth inning and McDermott, who was responsible for six of the 17 walks, faced Pat Seerey with a full count. Harris, who had given up 11 of those free passes, was cheering from the bench. "Throw it away, Mick," he yelled to his young teammate. "We'll break the record."

McDermott responded by throwing a fastball a foot above the batter's head for what should have been a walk. But Seerey, who seldom saw a pitch he didn't like, swung and missed.

So McDermott had a strikeout, instead of the record-setting walk.

CHAPTER 2

STRANGE INJURIES

Athletes are no strangers to injuries, but every once in awhile an injury can change a career or create some laughs at a player's expense. Here are a few of the more unusual.

Relay Throw Beans Dean

Jerome "Dizzy" Dean, one of baseball's greatest pitchers, was also one of its greatest characters. When his team, the St. Louis Cardinals, faced the Detroit Tigers in the 1934 World Series, the ever-confident Dizzy predicted that, between them, he and his brother "Daffy" would win all four games for the world championship. Coming into the fourth game, the brothers had each won one game, and the Cardinals led the Series, two games to one.

In the fourth inning of the fourth contest, Dizzy, who was not pitching that day, was put into the game to pinch run for slow-moving Virgil "Spud" Davis. On the first pitch, the next batter, Pepper Martin, hit a ground ball to Tiger second baseman Charlie Gehringer, who threw to shortstop Bill Rogell, covering second, for the force-out. Dizzy came running into the bag standing up, trying to prevent a double play. Rogell's relay throw hit him squarely in the forehead, knocking Dizzy unconscious.

Dean was revived after reaching the clubhouse, and his first words after coming to were to ask whether the Tigers had gotten Martin at first. An X ray taken at St. John's hospital revealed no fracture and, to add insult to injury, the next morning's newspaper ran the following headline:

"DEAN'S HEAD X-RAYED: SHOWED NOTHING."

Remarkably, Dean showed up the next day to pitch as scheduled. A good sport, he posed with Rogell for photographs, shook his hand, and placed an arm around his shoulders. He even removed his cap to show the bump raised by Rogell's throw. Dizzy smilingly accepted a fan's gift of a freshly painted steel army helmet and promised to wear it whenever he ran bases.

Dean pitched, but lost the game, 3–1. Then brother Daffy pitched the Cardinals to victory in the sixth game, again tying the series. Dizzy pitched the seventh game and won, 11–0, giving St. Louis the championship. True to Dizzy's prediction, the Dean brothers had accounted for all four Cardinal victories.

Injuries Off the Field

Sometimes players get strange injuries off the field that keep them out of the game. For example, in August 1987, Greg Harris, a Texas Rangers pitcher who wasn't on the mound that day, kept tossing sunflower seeds to a friend in the stands from the steps of the dugout. This made his elbow so sore he had to miss two pitching starts. And when Wade Boggs was playing third base for the Boston Red Sox, he missed a week during the 1986 season. This was because he bruised his ribs when he fell while trying to pull off his cowboy boots!

No Way to Treat a Mom!

It seemed like the ideal way to spend Mother's Day.

On May 14, 1939, in Comiskey Park, Chicago, Bob "Rapid Robert" Feller was pitching for the visiting Cleveland Indians against the White Sox. Seated in the stands above the first-base dugout were Bob's mother, father, and sister.

In the third inning, Chicago third baseman Marv Owen, a right-handed batter, got around late on a fast ball and fouled it sharply into the stands. Defying all odds, the ball struck none other than Mrs. Feller, just above the right eye. The blow shattered her glasses, leaving her with a deep cut that required six stitches.

What a way to spend Mother's Day!

The game was stopped for ten minutes as Bob and others rushed to her side. Once assured his mother would be okay, Bob resumed pitching, and with Ben Chapman batting in seven runs with two homers and a triple, Feller and the Indians won the game, 9–4.

Her experience didn't sour Mrs. Feller on the ballpark. On Opening Day of the next season, April 16, 1940, she sat in the very same seat at Comiskey Park, to watch her son pitch again against the White Sox.

Would lightning strike again?

As matters turned out, this time the lightning was from Bob's arm, and the "strikes" were those he threw past opposing batters. Mrs. Feller's courage in tempting fate was rewarded, as her son recorded the only Opening Day no-hitter in modern Major League baseball history, 1–0, and really made his mother's day.

Never Ask for a Day Off

Everybody needs a day off from work once in awhile. But if the fellow who replaces you is a rising star determined not to skip a day, that one day can put a crimp in your career.

Take the case of first baseman Wally Pipp, who played for the New York Yankees. On June 1, 1925, he was hit in the head during batting practice by a fastball. As a result, Pipp didn't play in that day's game—and he never started another game at first base again. The reason? The man who replaced Wally was a talented rookie slugger named Lou Gehrig, who went on to establish a consecutive-game playing streak of 2,130 games.

Gehrig's consecutive game streak was broken by the Baltimore Orioles Cal Ripken, Jr., who played 2,632 games in a row before finally taking a well-deserved day off.

Butt Really

Clarence Blethen of the Red Sox liked to pitch toothless to look mean and to frighten batters. He used to take out his false teeth and keep them in his back pocket. This tactic turned on him when, during one game in 1923, he slid into second base and his own teeth bit him on the butt!

CHAPTER

3

IN A LEAGUE OF THEIR OWN

Fans come in all shapes and sizes. Many are knowledgeable about the sports they follow. Some fans are serious, some are funny. And some are so outrageous, they're simply in a league of their own.

One of My Best Fans

Outfielder Andy Van Slyke, who played with the St. Louis Cardinals and then the Pittsburgh Pirates, described the difference between playing at home and on the road. "On the road," he explained, "when you go downstairs for coffee in your underwear, they throw you out of the kitchen."

And after a very frustrating day at home plate, he said, referring to a popular movie at the time, "I couldn't have driven Miss Daisy home today." But when he was asked whether there was anyone with whom he'd trade places for a day: "My wife. So I could see how wonderful it is to live with me."

A Fan to the End

Betty Fein was such an avid fan of Mickey Mantle and the New York Yankees, she once trained her pet parakeet to say, "Go Mickey. Go Yankees."

Then she told her grandson, Eddie Ellner, that if the Yankees ever won a pennant again, she'd like to have her ashes scattered at Yankee Stadium. At first, her grandson thought she was kidding, but she convinced him she wasn't.

Mrs. Fein died in 1990 at the age of 83. After the Yankees won the World Series in

1996, Eddie and his brother finally did what he called "this insane thing." Without permission of the team, they scattered her ashes from a marble urn along the first-base line, near the Yankee dugout, and on home plate.

A Fein tribute.

A Fan-tastic Parade of Pitchers

What can a baseball team that's already lost a hundred games in the season do for its fans? How can the team repay such loyalty? After losing 100 games during the 1949 season, the St. Louis Browns came up with an interesting idea.

The club announced that on the last day of the regular season it would use nine pitchers against the Chicago White Sox—whether they were needed or not.

The reason, a club spokesman said, was that it would give fans a chance to have a last look at each hurler. The team had ten pitchers on the roster, he said, and might use the tenth man, as well.

True to their promise, the Browns called on nine different pitchers in the opener of a last-day doubleheader with the White Sox, who got hits against all but one of the Browns hurlers and won 4–3.

Maybe less is more. Because in the bottom of the doubleheader, the Browns, using just one pitcher, won 5–3. They concluded the season with a record of 53 victories and 101 defeats, 44 games out of first place. Despite the dismal record, they were not in last place. The Browns finished seventh, three games better than the cellar-dwelling Washington Senators, whose record was 50–104.

Anything for a Ball!

Every fan loves catching a baseball at a game, but not many would go to the extremes that actor Charlie Sheen did in hopes of catching a home run ball.

For an April 1996 game in Anaheim Stadium between the California Angels and the Detroit Tigers, Sheen spent $6,500 to buy out 20 rows of seats behind the left field fence—2,615 tickets —so that he and three friends could get to any home run balls hit without any interference from other fans. "I didn't want to crawl over the paying public," he told a sports magazine. "I wanted to avoid the violence."

He avoided the violence, all right. But it seems he also avoided getting any baseballs, because no home run was hit in his direction.

Who Says Lightning Never Strikes Twice!

Maybe Charlie Sheen should have sat near Chicago Cubs fan Matt Kramer.

On Opening Day at Wrigley Field in 1994, the Mets hit two homers to right field in the third inning (by José Vizcaino and Todd Hundley) and, amazingly, the same fan—Matt Kramer—caught both home run balls. And, as good Cub fans do with home run balls hit by opposing players, he returned them to the field.

Kramer's luck earned him a spot that week on *The Late Show with David Letterman*.

Just Catching the Ball Is Reward Enough

A fan willing to give up a ball he or she has caught can find it profitable, if the ball is a record setter.

The man who caught Roger Maris' then record-breaking 61st home run in 1961, Sal Durante, offered to give Roger the baseball. But Maris suggested, "Keep it and make some money."

He did. In exchange for the ball, a restaurant owner gave Sal $5,000 and two trips to the West Coast.

Note: Mark McGwire's record-setting 70th home run ball was auctioned off for slightly over three million dollars!

Ad-dieu to His Friends

Some athletes relate particularly well to their fans.

After pitcher Jim Abbott was released by the California Angels early in 1997, he bought ads in two southern California newspapers, which said:

"Angel Fans...Thanks For The Cheers... Thanks For The Jeers...Thanks For The Memories....All My Best—Jim Abbott."

Getting Their Goat

When a team loses, one player who has a particularly poor game is usually labeled the "goat." But that doesn't necessarily mean a club should ban *real* goats from the ballpark!

Yet that's what happened when a fan named Billy "Goat" Sianis wanted to attend a 1945 World Series game at Wrigley Field with his pet goat. Chicago Cub officials wouldn't allow the animal inside the stadium, so Billy angrily responded by putting a "goat curse" on the Cubs so they'd never win a World Series.

It wasn't until 1984 that the Cubs finished in first place again. And earlier that year, they had invited Sianis' nephew and the original goat's distant cousin to Opening Day at Wrigley Field.

No kid-ding.

Window Pain

It was a shattering experience—especially for someone who wasn't a fan.

When Sammy Sosa of the Chicago Cubs hit a long homer on May 5, 1996, the ball flew out the park and went through the window of a man who lived across the street from Wrigley Field!

Philippe Guichoux, the apartment dweller whose window felt the pain of Sosa's blast, had recently moved to Chicago from France. He said he had known the apartment was near a field. "I just didn't know baseballs would go out of the field." He obviously did not know the home-run legend Sammy Sosa played for the Cubs.

Shots Heard 'Round the World

Bobby Thomson's historic two-out, three-run homer in October 1951 defeated the Brooklyn Dodgers in the bottom of the ninth inning of the third and decisive play-off game, and gave his New York Giants the National League pennant. It became known as the "shot heard 'round the world."

Here is the odd part. The dramatic blast occurred during the Korean conflict. Reports say that one Giant fan was on combat duty in Korea with a U.S. Army unit that was dug in around a hill waiting for the command to attack it. When the fan heard the news of Thomson's homer on Armed Forces Radio, he got so excited, he started yelling and jumping up and down. His fellow soldiers thought his actions were the signal to attack, and they proceeded to launch a blistering assault on a hill, where, it turned out, there was no enemy.

Writing later about what that fan's reaction had triggered, sports columnist Phil Mushnick appropriately called the events surrounding the Thomson blast "shots heard 'round the world."

They'll Never Learn

Home openers at 19 Major League ballparks for the 1997 season were to feature giveaways of baseballs to fans. But after the openers in Milwaukee and Kansas City were delayed by fans throwing the free balls onto the field, the acting commissioner ordered that teams not give out balls before the games.

The game in Milwaukee, in which the Brewers beat the Texas Rangers, 5–3, was delayed three times. Texas manager Johnny Oates pulled his players off the field twice in the second inning and played the game under protest.

Balloons, Cowbells, and Other Strange Music

The Brooklyn Dodgers attracted some wild fans. One, Eddie the Milkman, released balloons to celebrate the feats of his hero, Cookie Lavagetto.

Another was Hilda Chester, who attended every game at Brooklyn's Ebbets Field for more than 30 years. She heartily cheered on her favorites and jeered the opposition with a frying pan and iron ladle, and later a cowbell.

More music was provided by the "Dodger Sym-phoney," a group of drummers, trumpeters, and cymbal-players who loudly expressed their feelings—with renditions of "Three Blind Mice" when the umpires ruled against the Dodgers and "The Worms Crawl In" when opposing players returned to the dugout after making an out.

Dressed for the Occasion

After Tug McGraw, relief pitcher for the New York Mets, had thrown at and hit Dodger Bill Russell in Los Angeles, touching off a brawl, he came up with a plan to win over the fans.

The next time Tug was at Dodger Stadium, he came out for batting practice wearing a military fatigue outfit and combat helmet. Russell put on an oversized, comic boxing glove. The fans were delighted.

Fair Catch?

Sometimes a fan does more than root for his or her favorite team. One 12-year-old Little Leaguer arguably helped the New York Yankees win the American League pennant!

In the bottom of the eighth inning of the first game of the 1996 American League Championship series, the Yankees trailed the Baltimore Orioles by a run, 4–3. Derek Jeter, the Yankee shortstop, hit a long fly ball to right and as Tony Tarasco, the Baltimore right fielder, backed up to camp under it on the warning track, the young fan wearing a baseball glove leaned over and touched the ball. "It was a magic trick," Tarasco said, "because the ball just disappeared out of midair."

Was it fan interference? The Orioles thought so. But Rich Garcia, the umpire who was on the right-field line, ruled it a home run. After watching a replay on television, he was asked whether he still thought it was a home run. Garcia answered, "After looking at it, no, obviously...It probably was a situation where the ball would have hit the wall." Meanwhile Tarasco said the reason he didn't jump for the ball was because it was about to settle into his glove.

It's against the rules to protest an

umpire's judgment, but the Orioles claimed there was an allowable exception to appealing the umpire's decision: If one is "convinced that it is in violation of one of the rules." The rule in question says if fan interference prevents a fielder from catching a ball "the umpire shall declare the batter out."

Baltimore appealed to league president Gene Budig and acting baseball commissioner Bud Selig to "preserve the integrity of the game" by reversing the umpire's decision, and having the game replayed from the eighth inning. But the game-tying home run was upheld. The Yankees won, 5–4, in the 11th inning on an undisputed homer by Bernie Williams, and went on to take the American League Championship and then the World Series.

The fan, 12-year-old Jeffrey Maier, was treated as a hero by some, a villain by others. "I'm a Yankees fan," he explained. "But I didn't mean to do anything to change the outcome of the game or do anything bad to the Orioles. I didn't think anything like this would ever happen to me. It's pretty cool. I feel bad for Baltimore fans, but for Yankee fans, if I helped the team, it's pretty good."

DON'T LET IT GET YOU DOWN

Athletes have different ways of dealing with anger, defeat, or disappointment. Sometimes they're funny, sometimes they're not, and sometimes they have to pay for their actions.

Bat Trick

The Dodgers' Zack Wheat, a man known for his high batting averages, was seldom called upon to bunt. But this time he was at the plate in a situation that cried out for a bunt.

Wheat kept looking to manager Wilbert Robinson, who was coaching at third at the time, for the bunt sign, but Robinson just stared blankly into space. Zack kept trying to stall until he got the sign, but Robinson had forgotten how to signal for a bunt. Finally Robinson, in pantomime, acted out a batter bunting the ball.

At this, Wheat got so angry that he swung at the first pitch and hit the ball out for a home run. As he rounded third, Robinson patted him and said, "Attaboy, Zack, that's the way to hit 'em." He'd not only forgotten the bunt sign, but also the fact that Zack had disobeyed his orders!

Home Run? That's Fine

Unlike Zack Wheat and Wilbert Robinson, when Red Murray hit a home run for the New York Giants in the early 1900s, his manager, John McGraw, didn't congratulate him. He fined him!

"When I saw that fat pitch coming to me,

I just knew I had to belt it," Murray explained. But the explanation didn't pacify McGraw, a stickler for rules, who had ordered Murray to bunt.

Foli's Folly

Did he count curveballs to fall asleep?

After shortstop Tim Foli, then a minor-leaguer with Visalia in the California League, went hitless in a doubleheader, he was so angry he went back to his apartment, took a blanket and pillow, went back to the ballpark and slept overnight in the infield at the shortstop position.

He probably dreamt of extra-base hits.

Hold the Mayo

Sometimes it pays to argue.

Denny McLain was pitching against the Boston Red Sox on August 16, 1968, with the Detroit Tigers leading, 2–0. With Red Sox runners on second and third, Tiger manager Mayo Smith told McLain to walk the batter, Dalton Jones, but McLain refused. "I'm not walking anybody."

He struck out Jones on three pitches. Up came Carl Yastrzemski, and down he went—on three pitches. Next batter was Ken Harrelson, and again the manager wanted the batter walked, but McLain was adamant. "You must be out of your mind," he told Smith. "He hasn't hit me since he came into the League." On three sliders, McLain struck Harrelson out, retiring the side.

"Denny," said Smith, "we'll never have another argument on the mound."

Their Victory Suited Them

While Detroit trailed by half a dozen runs, the owner of the Tigers, Walter O. Briggs, Sr., was getting a shave and listening to the game on the radio. He told the barber, "If we win today, I'm going to buy every one of the ballplayers a new suit."

It seemed like a safe enough promise, but the Tigers went on to win the game. Briggs kept his promise. He ordered a suit from his private tailor for each of the Tigers.

The Umpire Didn't Dig It

People have some odd ways of protesting calls by the officials.

George Weiss, then president of the New Haven baseball club in the Eastern League, used to sit in the owner's box in Weiss Park. The box was very close to the field, and once when an umpire called a ball fair that Weiss considered to have been foul by more than a foot, George complained bitterly.

When the ump refused to reverse his decision, Weiss took a shovel and lifted up a section of the playing field, revealing the dent supposedly made by the ball, which, according to Weiss, was well outside the line.

The Faint of Heart

Once, to protest an umpire's call, Mets manager Casey Stengel pretended to faint. The umpire, Beans Reardon, didn't "fall" for the trick. As Casey lay on the ground,

Beans fell to the ground, too. Stengel knew he'd been upstaged.

Cone-fused

On a ball hit to the infield when he was a pitcher with the New York Mets, David Cone covered first and was so upset with umpire Charlie Williams for calling the batter safe, he forgot to call time as he argued. And while he objected, two runners scored!

Early Dismissal

In this case, a player used "bad behavior" and an early dismissal by an umpire to his advantage.

Like most players on teams not in the race for the pennant, Detroit pitcher Frank Lary was anxious to go home. On the day of the last game of the season, Lary, who wasn't scheduled to pitch, had booked a three-o'clock flight home, although his team's game was due to start at two.

Lary told Umpire Ed Runge about his flight plight and asked if he could get him out of the game in time. The umpire said he'd try to help.

On the first pitch of the game, Runge

called a strike, and Lary, who was standing on the top step of the dugout, yelled, "Hey, Runge, what kind of a call is that? You trying to make a quick getaway?"

"You're out of the game," Runge said, pointing at him.

"Thanks," said Lary, who took off on his own quick getaway—his flight home.

Don't Get Mad, Get Even

Sometimes a pitcher in a tight spot welcomes a chance to relax. But not always.

With two runners on base and no outs, Bob Uecker, then the Braves catcher, came out to give his pitcher, Lew Burdette, a breather. But the hurler was unhappy about it; he was concerned the crowd would think Uecker was giving him advice.

So Burdette gave Uecker a piece of his mind: "The only thing you know about pitching," Burdette snarled, "is that you can't hit it."

Uecker meekly went back behind the plate. But he got even: He told the batter what the next pitch was going to be.

CHAPTER

5

JUST WHAT YOU'D HEX-PECT

Sometimes athletes, fans, and managers try to manufacture their own good luck—or avoid bad luck—in the oddest ways. Using magic charms, strange rituals, special clothing, or favorite equipment, they hope to tip the scales of luck in their favor.

Sharp-Eyed Bat

When a grounder makes its way through a small opening between fielders, it's sometimes said that "the ball had eyes." Seldom is vision attributed to bats. Yet Forrest "Spook" Jacobs used to squirt eyedrops on his bat before a game. Jacobs, who played with the Philadelphia Athletics and Kansas City Royals in the mid-1950s, explained that he did it so he'd have a "seeing-eye" bat.

Some Batty Beliefs

If you've read Bernard Malamud's novel *The Natural* or have seen the movie with Robert Redford in the title role, you'll remember that his bat, "Wonderboy," had incredible powers. Well some real-life baseball players have attributed magical power to their bats, too.

John "Chief" Meyers, an old-time catcher for the Giants and Dodgers in the early 1900s believed each bat contained exactly 100 hits, so no other player had better dare use his. A teammate, Benny Kauff, felt that bats grew tired, so he rested them often.

Carlton Fisk, home-run hitting catcher for the Red Sox and White Sox from 1969 to 1993, would not put his bats in the dugout rack with his teammates' bats. He'd store them in his locker and carry them in his own bag. Rather than allow an equipment manager or batboy to bring his bats from the locker room in the dugout, he'd do it himself.

Mark Grace, first baseman for the Chicago Cubs, used a designated "bat sitter"—a teammate to hold his bats when he wasn't available himself.

Friendly Gestures

Sammy Sosa, slugger of the Chicago Cubs, is a friendly fellow. In the first inning of every game, on his way to the plate, he taps the umpire and the catcher on the back of the leg—just to say hello.

Hair of the Dog

During batting practice before a game against visiting Pittsburgh, Marge Schott, the Cincinnati Reds' controversial former owner, slipped wads of dog hair into the back pockets of four players for good luck, but it wasn't enough. The Reds suffered their eighth consecutive loss, 10–7.

Uniformly Unlucky

When the Chicago Cubs won the National League pennant in 1929, the team's owner, William Wrigley, ordered new uniforms for his players to wear in the World Series against the Philadelphia Athletics. The players objected, fearing it would be bad luck to abandon the uniforms they'd worn through the long, tough race for the pennant.

So Wrigley had the old uniforms dry-cleaned instead. Maybe he should have skipped the cleaning, because the Cubs lost the Series, four games to one. If they'd worn the new uniforms, they could have blamed them for the loss.

Uniformly Superstitious

Often, sports personalities find luck in clothing, wearing special items or, during a winning streak, making no changes in wardrobe. Check some of these players out.

When playing well, shortstop Walt Weiss didn't like to change a thing. He even wore the same white University of North Carolina at Chapel Hill wrestling T-shirt and a left sock with a hole in it.

Rob Murphy, a Cincinnati Reds pitcher in the 1980s, took the mound only when he wore his black silk underwear. "I look at it as my security blanket." But if his pitching took a bad turn, Murphy admitted, "I'd take it off in a minute."

Under his uniform, Luis Tiant, a pitcher from 1964 to 1982, liked to smoke cigars in the shower and wore a special loincloth around his waist "to ward off evil."

The Salt Lake Trappers, a minor league team in Utah, never washed or changed their socks during a 29-game winning streak in 1987.

After the Boston Red Sox lost the 1978 American League East playoff game to the New York Yankees on Bucky Dent's home run, they stopped wearing red hats, and didn't resume wearing them until April 1997.

A Really Hot Streak

When the Chicago White Sox played the Boston Red Sox in a game in 1982, it was so cold that Chicago's manager, Tony LaRussa, wore his heavy wool winter jacket. The White Sox won the game, so LaRussa decided to keep wearing the heavy jacket. He wore it during every game played in the next three weeks, including two games when the temperature reached 90 degrees. During the time LaRussa dressed warm, the White Sox won 15 and lost three.

To the Showers

When pitchers are taken out of a game,
they're said to have been sent "to the show-
ers." Joaquin Andujar sometimes jumped
into the shower after a game he lost — while
wearing his uniform! Andujar explained
that he wanted "to wash the bad out of it."

Lucky Pants

Sometimes good luck comes from another player's clothing.

When the 1987 baseball season opened, the New York Mets' ace pitcher, Dwight "Doc" Gooden was out of the lineup, involved in a rehabilitation program.

His close friend and teammate, Darryl Strawberry, was very disturbed by Doc's predicament, and announced he was dedicating the season to Gooden and to his own son, Darryl Strawberry, Jr.

On Opening Day, April 7, at a game that Gooden ordinarily would have pitched, Darryl wore Doc's uniform pants. "I'm very comfortable in them," Strawberry commented. "I wish I could have worn the whole uniform. I'm very close to Dwight."

Whether it was the fact he was wearing Doc's pants or his own great hitting ability, Strawberry was the hero of the game. Mookie Wilson singled to open the action for the Mets. Tim Teufel then flied out but was awarded first base when the umpire ruled catcher Junior Ortiz of the Pirates guilty of interference. Pirate pitcher Bob Patterson retired the next two Mets, Keith Hernandez and Gary Carter. If not for the interference, those outs would have retired the side. But given the "extra" out, Strawberry came to the plate and belted a two-run homer. The Mets won the game, 3–2.

The Name of the Game

Tito Fuentes, who was nicknamed "Parakeet" because he talked to everyone while on base, wore more than a dozen chains under his uniform, perfectly aligned. Before a game, he'd coat his body with chalk and grease. Tito, an infielder for several teams, including the San Franciso Giants, was afraid of being touched by anybody trying to break up a double play.

He named one of his sons "Clinch" because he was born the day before the Giants clinched the division title in 1971. It could have been worse. If the Giants had made it to the World Series and the baby had been born then, Tito said, "I was going to name him W. S."

Winning Rituals

Rituals have always been a favorite of the superstitious for coaxing luck to come their way. Athletes are no exception. You might be surprised at some of the rituals they count on to bring them good fortune.

As an infielder and then as manager for several teams, Leo Durocher would not change his clothes during a winning streak, and he'd ride in the back of the bus to break a losing streak. In the ninth inning, if his team was ahead, he'd walk the length of the dugout for a drink of water after each out registered by his opponents.

Mark McGwire always puts on his uniform in the same order—socks, then pants, then shirt. And he always steps out of the clubhouse for batting practice with his right foot first, and returns to the clubhouse with his left foot first.

Some players make sure they touch second base on the way to the dugout. Willie Mays was among them, but he added his own custom of kicking the sack.

The great tap dancer Bill "Bojangles" Robinson used to help out his favorite team, the Yankees, by doing a little dance and then scattering "gooferdust" he carried in a vial. He'd spread the dust on New York bats to encourage hits and on New York gloves to avert errors.

Vic Davalillo believed in petting baby chicks before a game. He played baseball from 1963 to 1980 with various ballclubs, including the Cleveland Indians, Pittsburgh Pirates, and Los Angeles Dodgers.

When he was on a winning streak, Al Lopez, the Hall of Fame manager who caught from 1928 to 1947 for the Dodgers, Braves, Pirates, and Indians, used to eat the same meal he did on the days of the streak. Once he had a breakfast of kippered herring and eggs 17 days in a row.

Yankee shortstop Phil "Scooter" Rizzuto used to put a wad of gum on the button of his cap, and remove it only after a Yankee loss.

Hex-Breakers

Major league ballplayers also had their favorite methods to break hexes. Ernie Koy made sure to get up from the right side of the bed; Reggie Smith would burn incense; Rico Carty would rub his bat with "magic" oil; and George Stallings would trim his catcher's mustache.

Playing the Clock

In some sports, a team that's ahead will "play the clock," using up as much time remaining in the game as possible. That doesn't work in baseball, which doesn't operate on a time basis.

But Arthur Weaver, who played baseball in the early 1900s when teams played all their games before darkness fell, got his nickname "Six O'clock" from the fact that he considered it unlucky to keep playing after six P.M. If the game was still in progress when the clock struck six, he'd immediately leave the field.

The first official Major League night game was played on May 24, 1935, in Cincinnati. The Cincinnati Reds defeated the Philadelphia Phillies, 2–1. President Franklin D. Roosevelt threw the switch at the White House to turn on the lights. The first night game in the American League was played at Philadelphia's Shibe Park on May 16, 1939. The Cleveland Indians defeated the Philadelphia A's, 8–3, in ten innings.

For the Birds

George Stallings, who managed the Boston Braves of 1914 to their "miracle" pennant (rising from last place on July 19) and World Series sweep over the Philadelphia Athletics, was very superstitious.

It bothered him to see sparrows land on the turf in front of the players' bench, and so he carried a supply of pebbles to throw at the birds to scatter them. The players, knowing their skipper's dislike of the sparrows, often would sprinkle oats to attract them.

When Stallings ran out of pebbles, he'd assign a sub to sit on the dugout steps and pound the turf with a bat to drive the birds away.

Stallings also believed that scraps of

paper were an evil omen, so he ordered that the area in front of the dugout be kept clear of them. Many fans, aware of his dislike of paper, kept throwing torn paper on the field just to irritate him.

Stallings used to assign Joe Oeschger, a regular churchgoer, to pitch on Sundays, figuring he'd be on the side of the angels. But in the time they were together, Joe's won-loss record was only 19–15.

Watch Your Step

Many baseball players refuse to step on a foul line.

One of them, Mel Stottlemyre, former ace hurler for the Yankees (1964–74), explained how he came to believe even more strongly in this superstition.

One day, headed for the bullpen to warm up before the start of a game against the Minnesota Twins, he avoided the foul line, as was his custom. But Jim Hegan, a Yankee coach, urged him not to be superstitious and to step on the line, not avoid it. So Mel did just that.

But he quickly regretted his action. The first batter he faced, Ted Uhlaender, lined a single off Stottlemyre's left shin. Rod Carew, Tony Oliva, and Harmon Killebrew followed with extra base hits and the next man singled and scored, and Mel was charged with five runs. "I haven't stepped on a foul line since," he said.

But one foul line avoider, Darrell Porter, had second thoughts. Once, he said, "I accidentally did step on a line, and nothing bad happened. So now I make it a point, every year, of mashing that foul line with both feet when I go out there for introductions on opening day."

Whatever works.

CHAPTER

6

WE ARE FAMILY

Members of the same family have played professional sports together, some of them in pretty spectacular fashion. Here are some family combinations that have made history together.

Like Father, Like Son

Ken Griffey, Sr. and Ken Griffey, Jr. were the only father-son combination ever to play for the same major league baseball team (the Seattle Mariners) at the same time (from August of the 1990 season through part of 1991).

And they didn't just play together, they hit together. In the first inning of a game at California on September 14, 1990, the Griffeys hit back-to-back homers off Kirk McCaskill.

When he was in high school, Ken, Jr. was too nervous to play in front of his father. A-parent-ly, he got over his anxiety by the time he got to the Mariners.

What Ever Happened to Brotherly Love?

Brothers Joe, Dom, and Vince DiMaggio played in the big leagues at the same time, but for different teams. In 1941, in the midst of Joe DiMaggio's 56-game hit streak, he was robbed of a hit by a Boston Red Sox outfielder—his brother, Dom DiMaggio. Next time up, though, Joe homered, to keep the streak going.

During Joe's streak of getting at least one

base hit in 56 straight games, he scored 56 runs and missed by only one run of driving in 56. During the streak, he batted .408 on 91 hits against 42 pitchers. The day after that streak was halted, Joe started another streak that lasted 16 games. So in a stretch of 73 games he'd hit safely in 72.

I Want to Grow Up to Be Like Dad...and Grandad

At least three families have had three generations of baseball players: Ray Boone, his son Bob Boone, and grandsons Bret and Aaron Boone; Gus Bell, his son Buddy Bell, and grandson David Bell; and Sam Hairston and his son and grandson, both named Jerry.

30-30 Club Members

Bobby Bonds and Barry Bonds were the only father–son combo to have been both members of the 30-30 club, hitting 30 homers and stealing 30 bases in the same season.

All in the Family

On September 5, 1963, three Alou brothers—Felipe, Matty, and Jesus—played in the San Francisco Giants outfield at the same time. The Giants beat the Pirates that game, 13–5.

Come On, Coach, Give Me a Chance

It helps to be the supervisor as well as the employee.

Late in his career, Warren Spahn was both pitching coach and pitcher for the New York Mets and was eager to prove he could pitch a full nine innings.

In a game against the Dodgers, he had a 3–0 lead in the ninth inning, but the Dodgers scored twice and had runners at first and third with no outs. Coming out to the mound, manager Casey Stengel spoke to Spahn in his capacity as pitching coach. Casey asked him which relief pitcher he wanted to come in from the bullpen. Spahn said he preferred to stay with the starting pitcher (himself), and Stengel relented. Spahn retired the next three men.

Series Stott-ers

Todd Stottlemyre's start of a World Series game in 1993 for the Toronto Blue Jays made World Series history. He became the first son of a World Series starting pitcher to start a Series game. His father, Mel Stottlemyre, made three Series starts for the New York Yankees in 1964.

Triply Out of Action

In the 1920s, Casey Stengel was president, manager, and right fielder of the Boston Braves' farm team in Worcester, Massachusetts. According to one writer, he got out of his triple responsibilities this way: as manager, he released Stengel the player; as president, he dismissed Stengel the manager; and as himself, he resigned as president.

CHAPTER

7

IT FIGURES

Statistics are a big part of sports. Sometimes athletes like to boast about their statistics and sometimes they'd rather forget about them. Some of the most interesting ones are those we don't generally pay attention to—and sometimes an athlete's claim to fame is a near miss at a record. But face it, either way, statistics are a big part of the enjoyment of sports, and they often do reflect major achievements. Here are some exceptional ones.

He Could Do It All

Before he became a full-time outfielder because of his hitting prowess, Babe Ruth was an outstanding pitcher. Playing for the Boston Red Sox, he played the outfield on days he wasn't pitching.

In World Series competition, he pitched 29 2/3 scoreless innings, a record that stood for more than 40 years until Whitey Ford of the New York Yankees ran up a streak of 33 2/3 scoreless World Series innings. In a game in the 1916 World Series against the Brooklyn Dodgers, Ruth not only pitched but drove in the winning run.

A Perfectly Fair Trade

Often trades are made involving a player "to be named later." Well, the personnel involved in this trade couldn't have been more equal.

On April 25, 1962, the Cleveland Indians traded Harry Chiti to the New York Mets for "a player to be named later." Chiti didn't do well for the Mets, so when it came time for them to send a player to the Indians on June 15, 1962, as their part of the trade, they sent Chiti.

He was the first player ever to be traded for himself.

How Many Pitchers Does It Take?

During the 1967 season, the New York Mets used 27 pitchers, but finished last.

In 1996, the Angels used 29 different pitchers. Chuck Finley, the Angels ace pitcher, cracked: "We must have gone through a couple of miles of thread, just sewing names on jerseys."

Twin Triple Play?

The Minnesota Twins pulled off twin triple plays in a single game for the first time in Major League history. The feat occurred on July 17, 1990, in a game they lost 1–0 to the Boston Red Sox at Fenway Park.

Both triple plays came on sharp grounders hit to third baseman Gary Gaetti, who then relayed the ball to second baseman Al Newman, who threw it on to first baseman Kent Hrbeck. Tom Brunansky hit into the first one in the fourth inning, with the bases loaded; Jody Reed hit into the second one in the eighth inning, with runners on first and second.

Not Your Average Celebration

When Jimmy Piersall, one of baseball's most popular oddballs, hit the 100th home run of his career on June 23, 1963, he did something that was guaranteed to call attention to his feat: He circled the bases running backward, as he'd previously promised.

In fact, Piersall wanted to run the bases in reverse order, but the umps wouldn't allow it!

Dallas Green, the pitcher who'd given up the home run, wasn't happy with Piersall's zany antics. Neither was the commissioner of baseball. The league quickly enacted a new rule requiring runners to face the bases as they run.

Double Value at Every Position

Being named Most Valuable Player is possibly baseball's proudest accomplishment. Being MVP twice in succession more than doubles the pleasure.

Through 1996, 11 major baseball players have won the MVP Award two seasons in a row, and they represent every field position.

Listed below are the players, their positions, teams, and years they won the award. What a team these eleven would make!

PLAYER	TEAM	POSITION	YEARS MVP
Jimmy Foxx	Athletics	First base	1932, 1933
Frank Thomas	White Sox	First base	1993, 1994
Joe Morgan	Reds	Second base	1975, 1976
Mike Schmidt	Phillies	Third base	1980, 1981
Ernie Banks	Cubs	Shortstop	1958, 1959
Barry Bonds	Giants	Left field	1992, 1993
Mickey Mantle	Yankees	Center field	1956, 1957
Roger Maris	Yankees	Right field	1960, 1961
Dale Murphy	Braves	Right field	1982, 1983
Yogi Berra	Yankees	Catcher	1954, 1955
Hal Newhouser	Tigers	Pitcher	1944, 1945

Last Chance

When the Mets beat the Cubs in the first game of a doubleheader in 1973, clinching the pennant, there was no need to play the second game. It was canceled, by mutual consent.

Veteran Milt Pappas, who was supposed to pitch the nightcap for the Cubs, was unhappy with the cancellation. That start would have been a bid for his 100th National League win, but umpire Augie Donatelli declared the game would not be played.

Pappas, who was warming up, stood with his hands on his hips, shaking his head, as if he knew he'd never get another shot at number 100. He was right; he never pitched again in the Majors.

A Retiring Kind of Guy

In the fifth inning of a 1920 World Series game between the Brooklyn Robins (as the Dodgers were then known) and Cleveland Indians, the Robins had runners on first and second (Otto Miller and Pete Kilduff) and none out.

When their left-handed spitballer Clarence Mitchell lined a ball to the right of second base, everyone took off at the crack of the bat—the runners and Indian second baseman Bill Wambsganss. Bill speared the ball with one hand to retire the batter, tagged second to double off Kilduff who'd lit out for third, and then tagged Miller, who was running for second.

It was an unassisted triple play, the only

one ever in a World Series. Cleveland won the game, 8–1, and the Series, five games to two. (From 1919 through 1921, a team needed to win five games to take the Series.)

Triple Steals

A triple steal, when three runners steal a base at the same time, is a great rarity, but on July 25, 1930, the Philadelphia Athletics had two triple steals against Cleveland, one in the first and one in the fourth. The first of the base "thieves" were Al Simmons, Bing Miler, and Dib Williams. The second one involved future Hall of Famers Mickey Cochrane, Simmons (again!), and Jimmy Foxx.

Now That's Respect, Maybe

Mel Ott, the New York Giants slugging outfielder, who used to lift his front foot as he started his swing, drew 100 or more walks seven seasons in a row.

He was so feared as a home-run hitter that he was once walked intentionally— with the bases loaded! It happened on the last day of the 1929 season (October 5), when Ott was tied with the Phillies' Chuck Klein for the league lead in home runs. In the first game of the doubleheader between the Giants and Phillies, Klein hit a homer, to take a one home-run lead. Then Philly pitchers walked Ott intentionally five straight times—the last with the bases loaded—presumably to protect Klein's home run lead. Klein ended the season with 43 four-baggers to Ott's 42.

Can't Get Worse

Bob Buhl, playing for the Braves and Cubs in 1962, had 70 official at-bats and no hits, for a .000 season's batting average. (A player needs at least 50 at-bats to qualify for the dubious honor of lowest batting average for a season.)

Beginner's Luck

Hoyt Wilhelm of the New York Giants not only won his first Major League game (in relief) at the Polo Grounds on April 23, 1952, but hit a home run in his first Major League at-bat. But what really hurt is that, although Wilhelm pitched in 1,070 games in the Majors, he never hit another homer.

Beginner's Luck Wears the Same Uniform

For five straight years, from 1992 through 1996, the National League's Rookie of the Year Award went to a Los Angeles Dodger. The winners were Eric Karros (1992), Mike Piazza (1993), Raul Mondesi (1994), Hideo Nomo (1995), and Todd Hollandsworth (1996).

Beginner's Yuck

Virgil "Fire" Trucks had a winning career as a pitcher, including two no-hitters. But his first Major League start in 1942, for the Detroit Tigers against the Boston Red Sox, was discouraging, to say the least.

Red Sox leadoff hitter Johnny Pesky singled on Virgil's first pitch. The second hitter, Bobby Doer, also hit Trucks' first pitch, this one for a double. Ted Williams, the next batter, hit Trucks' first pitch for another double.

At this point, Trucks recalled in a letter to author Seth Swirsky, the Detroit manager called time and came to the mound. He asked the catcher, "Doesn't Virgil have it today?" And the catcher replied, "How do I know? I haven't caught a pitch yet."

MVP, No Matter Where

Outfielder Frank Robinson was the only baseball competitor ever voted Most Valuable Player in both the National (1961, Reds) and American Leagues (1966, Orioles). The Hall of Famer, the first African-American to manage a Major League team, managed Cleveland—as player-manager—then San Francisco and Baltimore.

Not Clean Enough

Major League ballplayers are always looking for a base hit, but one great hitter once rejected a single credited to him.

Future Hall of Famer Paul Waner, a Pittsburgh Pirates star who was now with the Boston Braves, was one hit away from the elite category of Major Leaguers who had 3,000 career hits.

On June 17, 1942, in the second game of a doubleheader against Cincinnati, Paul's teammate Tommy Holmes was on first and Paul was at bat. The hit-and-run signal was flashed, and Holmes broke for second on the pitch. Eddie Joost, the Cincinnati shortstop, ran over to cover. When Waner hit the ball to the spot that Joost just vacated, Joost reversed direction and got his glove on the ball, but couldn't hold it. Holmes was safe at second and Waner at first.

The official scorer in the press box held up a finger indicating Waner had been credited with a single—his 3,000th hit. As the crowd roared in tribute to Waner, umpire Beans Reardon went over to first to give Waner the ball as a souvenir. But Paul, who was standing on the bag, shook his head and shouted "No, no!" in the direction of the press box. He wanted his record breaker to be a clean hit, so the scorer reluctantly changed the single to an error.

Two days later, Waner got his 3,000th official hit on a crisp single to center. He ended his career with 3,152 hits. It could have been 3,153.

Oh, Those Bases on Balls!

Baseball managers often get more upset about pitchers giving up walks than they do about yielding hits. And with good reason.

On April 22, 1959, the Chicago White Sox scored 11 runs—yes, 11—in the seventh inning on only one hit, a single! In that inning, they had 10 walks, five of them with the bases loaded, and one hit batsman, and their opponents, the Kansas City A's, made three errors. The Sox won, 20–6.

CHAPTER

8

WHAT ABOUT ALL THE GOOD THINGS THEY DID?

Even the best of athletes and teams have their off days, and sometimes the memory of a single flawed play or game may last longer and remain clearer than all their stand-out performances.

Here are a few examples of times when some athletes might have been better off staying in bed for the day.

Don't Break the Hand That Signs Your Checks

After a foul ball hit by Royals catcher Sal Fasano zoomed off of Jay Hinrichs, assistant general manager, and then broke the wrist of general manager, Herk Robinson, Hinrichs commented: "I'd be worried about next year's contract if I was Sal Fasano."

Did Babe Make His Point?

Can a batter really predict he'll hit a homer on a particular turn at the plate, point to where the shot will go—and then make good on his prophecy?

Well, the feat is still being debated more than 60 years later, but legend has it that Babe Ruth did just that in the third game of the 1932 Series, played October 1 in Chicago, between the New York Yankees and Chicago Cubs.

The Babe, who—until Hank Aaron—was baseball's all-time home run leader, loved to mix it up with the fans, and the great Yankee slugger had plenty of opportunity that day.

Even before the game, Cub fans had jeered at Ruth and his wife as they came from or went to their hotel. During batting practice, Cub fans tossed lemons at him (and he'd throw some back), but that didn't sour the Babe, who hit a two-run homer early in the game.

Then in the fourth inning, Ruth, who was playing left field instead of his usual right-field position, missed a shoestring catch on a drive by Billy Jurges. The misplay led to a Cub run and a tie score. Babe tipped his cap, good-naturedly acknowledging the fans' taunts.

When he came up to bat in the fourth inning, Ruth kept up a running debate with the Cub bench. "I never had so much fun in my life," he said later, referring to having both players and fans needling him at the same time. A lemon had to be swept away by the plate umpire.

The crowd responded to every pitch Charley Root made to Ruth, especially the strikes. Root threw a called strike, and Babe extended one finger to let the crowd know he knew where the count stood; Root threw another called strike, and Babe put out two fingers.

Then, with the count full, Babe made his history-making gesture. He waved his bat toward the centerfield bleachers as if to say he'd get back at the fans with a mighty home run to that location.

Root pitched. Ruth swung—and connected! The ball disappeared. He'd belted a home run to the very spot where he'd pointed.

As he rounded the bases, Ruth made comments to the Cub infielders, then waved to the Cub dugout.

The blast, Ruth's second homer of the game, was followed immediately by Lou Gehrig's four-bagger (his second of the day). The Yankees won, 7–5, and, with another victory in the following game, swept the Series.

Asleep at the Plate

It was a stunning play...literally.

The score in the fourth game of the 1939 World Series between the Cincinnati Reds and the New York Yankees was tied, 4–4, in the top of the 10th inning.

With two out, the Yankees had Frank Crosetti at third and Charley Keller at first. Joe DiMaggio laced a single to right field, scoring Crosetti. When right fielder Ival Goodman let the ball roll through him for an error, Keller kept running, racing to beat the relay throw to the plate. He slid hard into catcher Ernie Lombardi, a future Hall of Famer, knocking the ball out of his glove.

It was no time for a nap, but the dazed catcher, in pain, seemed to doze. As Keller touched the plate, DiMaggio was motoring around the bases. And when the seemingly slumbering, lumbering Lombardi simply squatted on the ground, not going after the ball that was just a few feet away, Joe also scored for the third run of the inning. The Yankees won the game, 7–4, for a four-game sweep of the Series.

He Meant Well

During the 1986 season, Boston Red Sox manager John McNamara would put in a defensive replacement for Bill Buckner at first base during the late innings.

But in the sixth game of the World Series, with the Sox close to a world championship over the New York Mets, he left Buckner in the game. The reasoning: The veteran player would be on the field to celebrate with his teammates when the Sox won the game and the Series. Sadly for the Sox, they won neither.

When, with two outs, a dribbler by Mookie Wilson of the Mets went through Buckner's legs, the Mets won the game and went on to take the Series, in seven games.

Two Errors and You're Out

In the 1973 World Series against the Mets, the A's substitute second baseman Mike Andrews made two costly errors in the 12th inning of game two. They led to three Met runs and a New York victory, 10–7, that tied the Series at a game each.

The A's owner, Charles Finley, had the team physician, Dr. Harry Walker, declare Andrews "physically unfit" to continue playing in the Series due to a chronic shoulder disability, and requested permission to replace him with infielder Manny Trillo.

Finley even "persuaded" Andrews to add a postscript to the letter, saying, "I agree with the above." Later Andrews, expressing regrets at having signed the letter, at first charged that Finley had "threatened to destroy me in baseball" unless he did sign, but then softened his comments.

Andrews' teammates were outraged at Finley's efforts to get rid of him, and some hinted at the possibility of refusing to play.

Several taped Andrews' number 17 to their sleeves, saying that it was "in memory of Mike Andrews."

The commissioner of baseball rejected Finley's request and commented that his action had "had the unfortunate effect of embarrassing a player who has given so many years of able service to professional baseball."

Andrews sat out the third game (won by the A's, 3–2, in 11 innings), then, apparently physically fit to play, came up to pinch-hit in the next game at the Mets' Shea Stadium. He received a standing ovation. When Andrews grounded out, he got a second ovation. Teammate Sal Bando shook his hand. The Mets won, tying the series at two games each, but the A's went on to win the Series, four games to three.

What Does a Fella Have to Do?

Harvey Haddix, then with the Pittsburgh Pirates, pitched 12 innings of perfect baseball against the Milwaukee Braves in a game on May 26, 1959, then lost the perfect game, the no-hitter, and the game on an unearned run in the 13th inning, by a score of 1–0.

That's Using Your Noggin

Managers and coaches are always telling their players to "keep your head in the game." But sometimes the advice boomerangs.

"Hey, I'm an entertainer," said José Canseco, then an outfielder with the Texas Rangers, after Carlos Martinez of the Cleveland Indians bounced a home run off his head and over the right-field fence in Cleveland on May 26, 1993.

It happened in the fourth inning when Canseco chased Martinez's lead-off fly to deep right. But when José turned his head to look for the wall, the ball grazed his glove, hit him in the head, and bounced over. "Anybody got a Band-Aid?" he joked later.

The noggin-assisted homer ignited a four-run inning and helping the Indians win, 7–6.

"I'll be on ESPN for about a month," José correctly predicted.

Not the Babe's Usual Ending

Babe Ruth was always a threat to end a ball game with a mighty home run. But this was one game he ended differently.

The St. Louis Cardinals led the New York Yankees, 3–2, in the seventh game of the 1926 World Series. To his surprise, the Cards' ace, Grover Cleveland Alexander, third-winningest pitcher in Major League history, was called in to relieve, after having won the sixth game for St. Louis.

Alexander struck out Tony Lazzeri with the bases loaded and two outs in the Yankee seventh. Then in the Yankee ninth inning, the Cards still leading, Babe Ruth walked with two outs. Bob Meusel was at bat, when, to everyone's amazement and the Yankees' regret, the great Bambino lit out for second base, only to be thrown out by Bob O'Farrell, the Cardinal catcher.

It was the only time the World Series had ended with a runner caught stealing. The Cards won the game, 3–2, and the Series, four games to three.

CHAPTER

9

GREAT PERFORMANCES

Some days are better than others. And some days are just plain great! Sometimes they even go down in history. Here are some examples of performances when these athletes showed off their very best.

Democracy in Action

The Chicago Cubs got just four hits in a game on September 5, 1969, against Steve Blass of the Pittsburgh Pirates. The unusual thing was that one player, Hall of Famer Billy Williams, got all of them—smacking two home runs and two doubles.

Billy got his hits off four different kinds of pitches—a fastball, curve, change-up, and slider—causing Blass to comment, "It was a very democratic day for him."

Work Hosses

In the years before jet travel and night games, athletes were a hardy lot whose stamina and drive could put some of today's players to shame. Here are some noteworthy examples:

Charles G. "Old Hoss" Radbourne, a pitcher for Providence in 1884, pitched the last 27 games of the season for his team—and won 26 of them! He had a 59–12 record for the regular season. Then he won three straight games in the World Series.

Nowadays, with baseball teams relying more and more on bullpen specialists, few pitchers get to pitch a complete game. But Joseph Jerome "Ironman" McGinnity, who in the off-season worked in an iron foundry, pitched five doubleheaders—and won both ends of the double bill three times in August 1903, en route to a 31-win season. In 1904, McGinty, who set the modern National League record for innings pitched in a season (434), won 35 games and lost eight as his New York Giants won the pennant.

Let's Play Some More

It's rare nowadays for baseball teams to play doubleheaders, but on October 2, 1920, two teams played a tripleheader! The Cincinnati Reds won the first two, 13–4 and 7–3, and the Pittsburgh Pirates won the third, 6–0. The finale was called after six innings because of darkness.

Hitting Pitchers

Many hitters would love to be able to pitch, and many pitchers wish they could be great hitters.

When the New York Mets played the Pittsburgh Pirates in a doubleheader in September 1969, the Mets won both games by a score of 1–0. In each game, it was a pitcher—Jerry Koosman in the first and

Don Cardwell in the second—who drove in the only run.

Neither hurler was known for his hitting ability.

Versatile Guy

Chicago Cub outfielder Doug Dascenzo got called on as a relief pitcher three times in 1991 and didn't allow a run.

Grand Style

Many a player has turned from goat to hero in the same game, but few have done it as quickly or dramatically as Bernie Williams of the New York Yankees.

In a game in Oakland on August 10, 1999, the Yankees had the bases loaded. Williams was at the plate. When he took a pitch for a ball, he trotted to first base, glad to be forcing in a run. But to his shock, Williams learned it was not ball four, but ball three.

Williams, mortified by "one of the most embarrassing moments of my career," returned to the plate, as teammates covered their faces to hide their laughter. The snickers quickly turned to cheers when, on the very next pitch, Williams drilled a grand slam. His homer capped an eight-run rally in a game the Yankees went on to win, 12–8. Chuckling about the mistake, Williams said: "If anybody on the team was going to do that, it was bound to be me. Because I'm the goofy one."

A Pretty Effective Pitch

One lesson that pitchers have pounded into them is to make every pitch count. How about this one?

In the fourth inning of the fourth game of the 1941 World Series, Larry French of the Brooklyn Dodgers came in to relieve against the New York Yankees, with two on and two out. Johnny Sturm was the runner on first and Phil Rizzuto on second.

French made just one pitch. And, although it was not swung at, fouled off, or hit safely, it still resulted in retiring the side.

The pitch was almost a wild one, but catcher Mickey Owen managed to block the ball far to his left. Seeing the runners break, he threw the ball to first baseman Dolph Camilli, who relayed the ball to third baseman Lew Riggs, who in turn threw to shortstop Pee Wee Reese, who chased down Rizzuto and tagged him out.

The Yankees won that game, 7–4, and took the next one, to win the Series in five games.

Rodeo Baseball

Former rodeo cowboy Tris Speaker, the star center fielder of the Boston Red Sox and Cleveland Indians, used to play his position so shallow he often made unassisted double plays at second base. No bull!

Making the Most of His Swings

Reggie Jackson's three consecutive home runs in the sixth and final game of the 1977 World Series were hit on three consecutive pitches off three different Dodger pitchers. Reggie's team, the Yankees, took the Series, four games to two.

Way to Lead Off

In 1996, Brady Anderson, Baltimore Orioles center fielder and lead-off batter, led off four games in a row with home runs. All in all, he had 12 lead-off homers for the season.

A great performance by a leading man.

So was this: As first in the batting order for the Oakland Athletics, Rickey Henderson led off both games of a doubleheader on July 5, 1993, with a home run. He was the first player to do that in 60 years.

Never Say Die

Talk about comebacks.

The Cleveland Indians had a 15–4 lead over the Philadelphia Athletics going into the bottom of the ninth in a game played June 15, 1925. A pretty comfortable lead, you'd think. But not comfortable enough. Because the Athletics scored 13 runs to win the game, 17–15.

Going Out With a Bang

May 25, 1935, on the last day of his Major League career, Babe Ruth, 40 years old and playing with the Boston Braves, clouted three home runs—the last one (number 714) was the first ball ever hit out of Pittsburgh's Forbes Field. It was estimated to have traveled 600 feet.

CHAPTER

10

IN THE
BEGINNING

*Did you ever wonder how baseball
used to be different from the way we
now know it, or how some of the tradi-
tions we take for granted got started?
What follows is some trivia about how
things used to be done, how they
changed, and even about some changes
that didn't stand the test of time.*

What, Me Slide?

In the earliest days of baseball, players didn't steal or slide. Ed Cuthbert of the Philadelphia Keystones was the first to steal a base, in 1865. Bob Addy of Rockford was the first to slide when stealing a base (1866). For a long time afterward, however, it was still considered unsportsmanlike.

In the 1880s, Chicago's Mike "King" Kelly was a player who not only loved to slide but seemed to be better at it than any other player of that period. In tribute, someone wrote a song, "Slide, Kelly, Slide!" a refrain youngsters would shout to each other for half a century after. Part of the lyrics: "Slide, Kelly! On your belly! Slide, Kelly, Slide!"

Not Seeing Is Still Believing

The man who wrote "Take Me Out to the Ball Game" had never seen a professional baseball game when in 1908 he wrote the song that would become a baseball classic.

Jack Norwood was inspired to write the number when he got on a train in New York and saw an ad promoting "baseball today" at the Polo Grounds.

And a Donut to Be Named Later

Athletes of years gone by were sometimes traded not for other players or money,
but for a product. For example:

Mike Dondero, a San Antonio infielder,
was traded in 1931 for a dozen donuts.

Jack Fenton, Memphis first baseman, was
traded to San Francisco for a box of prunes.

Charlie George was traded to Nashville
from Milwaukee in 1943 for a set of golf clubs.

Johnny Jones, a shortstop for Chattanooga,
was traded in 1931 for a turkey.

And in 1890, when he was still a minor

leaguer, Cy Young (who'd win 511 games in the Major Leagues, be elected to the Hall of Fame, and have the most desired award of Major League pitchers named after him) was sold to Cleveland by Canton for a suit. It was only fitting.

President-Setting Customs

In 1910, William Howard Taft was the first U.S. president to attend an opening-day baseball game and throw out the first ball to open the season, and he figures in one of the sport's legends.

It's long been a custom for baseball fans to stand up and stretch before the home team comes to bat in the bottom of the seventh inning. There are various theories about how the "seventh-inning stretch" came into being. A favorite one is that it started in 1910 when President Taft found his ballpark seat a bit confining for his 300-pound frame and stood up.

Out of respect for the President, who they thought was preparing to leave the ballpark, fans rose from their seats and originated the custom that remains today.

But there is evidence that the custom began many years before. Several of the theories center on the simple fact that around that time in the game, people were just tired of sitting. One belief is that the seventh inning was favored by the home fans for stretching because the number seven was considered lucky.

In April 1997, the Los Angeles Dodgers beat the New York Mets, 3–2, in a five-hour, 15-inning marathon at Los Angeles, and home fans stood for two seventh-inning stretches, in the seventh and 14th.

World Series, World War

The United States was at war September 5, 1918, when the Boston Red Sox and Cubs met in Chicago for the World Series.

During the seventh-inning stretch, the band suddenly started playing "The Star-Spangled Banner." Players faced the music, fans started singing, and by time the music finished, just about everyone was singing. The tune (which was not yet the country's official national anthem) was applauded and cheered.

The custom was repeated in every game of the Series, won in six games by the Red Sox (whose star pitcher, Babe Ruth, won two games). From then on, "The Star-Spangled Banner" became a traditional part of the national pastime. Beginning in 1942, with the United States again at war, it was played before all Major League games.

Yellow Ball

In the first game of a doubleheader at Brooklyn's Ebbets Field on August 2, 1938, the Dodgers and the visiting St. Louis Cardinals experimented with yellow baseballs instead of the standard white ones.

Johnny Mize of the Cardinals hit the first (and probably the last) Major League yellow-ball home run in history, but the Dodgers won, 6–2.

While many players and fans said the yellow balls were easier to see, a Dodger pitcher, Freddie Fitzsimmons, complained that the dye used to coat the balls came off on his hand. The second game was played with white balls. The experiment was tried three more times in 1939, but then the idea was dropped.

Elevating the Language

Cursing on the baseball field used to be fairly common, almost a second language. But Commissioner of Baseball Kenesaw "Mountain" Landis changed all that. In fact, in 1933, during the World Series, he fined umpire Bill Klem a day's pay for using an inappropriate word—not on the ball field but in a hotel elevator!

CHAPTER

11

THE LAST WORD

As they say in baseball, it ain't over til the fat lady sings. Well, folks, sad as it is, this book is nearly over. The fat lady is warming up her vocal chords, getting ready to burst into song. So here's a few famous quips to send you on your way!

"Aorta Read You the Book"

Yogi Berra and Bobby Brown were team-mates on the Newark Bears in 1946 and roomed together. One night they were reading in their room. Brown, a future cardiologist, was studying for a pathology exam he was due to take when he returned to medical school. Yogi was reading a Superman comic book. They finished their reading about the same time, and Yogi asked Bobby, "Well, how did yours come out?"

One Small Hit for Mankind

Like most pitchers, Gaylord Perry was far from being a power hitter. Alvin Dark, his manager one season on the San Francisco Giants, predicted sarcastically that there would be a man on the moon before Gaylord hit a home run.

Well, on July 20, 1969, Neil Armstrong of the Apollo 11 mission became the first man to walk on the moon. And just 17 minutes later—guess what—Garlord Perry hit the first homer of his Major League career!

Late Sleeper Excuse

Claudell Washington reported four days late to the Chicago White Sox in 1978, after being traded by the Texas Rangers. His reason? "I overslept."

Spanish-Speaking TV

Boston Red Sox outfielder Jeff Stone, returning home after playing in Latin America, left his TV set there. Asked why, he replied, "All the programs were in Spanish."

When invited to have a shrimp cocktail, he said, "No thanks, I don't drink."

Inspiration

Yogi Berra is represented in *Bartlett's Familiar Quotations* and elsewhere with such sayings as these:
- "Ninety percent of hitting is mental, the other half is physical."
- "When you come to the fork in the road, take it."
- "You can observe a lot by watching."
- "Nobody goes there anymore. It's too crowded."